CENTRAL BANKS AND WORLD MARKETS

How to Detect Early Warning Signals of Financial Distress

Fernando Walter Lolo and Cathal Rabbitte

© 2017 Fernando Walter Lolo and Cathal Rabbitte
www.DirectionalAlpha.com

ALL RIGHTS RESERVED. This book contains material protected under International and Federal Copyright Laws and Treaties. Any unauthorized reprint or use of this material is prohibited. No part of this book may be reproduced or transmitted in any form or by any means, electronic or mechanical, including photocopying, recording, or by any information storage and retrieval system without express written permission from the authors/publisher.

Copyright © 2017 Authored by Fernando Walter Lolo and Cathal Rabbitte

All rights reserved.

CONTENTS

A SPECIAL NOTE TO OUR READERS I

ABOUT THE AUTHORS III

DEDICATION IX

ACKNOWLEDGEMENTS X

INTRODUCTION 1

WHAT IS GROUPTHINK AND MARKET PSYCHOLOGY? 4

INTEREST RATES, CENTRAL BANKS, BONDS, YIELDS, BALANCE SHEETS 6

REFLATION, CHALLENGES, OPPORTUNITIES, AND EXPECTATIONS 11

WHY PAYRISES ARE IMPORTANT IN THE GENERATION OF ECONOMIC GROWTH 15

WHY THE FEDERAL RESERVE (FED) HAS CONTINUALLY FACED CHALLENGES SINCE THE LEHMAN BROTHERS COLLAPSE 20

CENTRAL BANKS, ASSETS, GOLD 25

THE REALITY OF DEFLATION IN THE EUROZONE AND ELSEWHERE 28

CAN THE FEDERAL RESERVE (FED) RAISE INTEREST RATES FURTHER? 33

THE EURO AND ITS ONGOING CHALLENGES 37

WHAT IS WRONG AT THE SYSTEM LEVEL? 43

CONCLUSION 54

DISCLAIMER 56

A SPECIAL NOTE TO OUR READERS

Dear Colleague,

Thank you for claiming your copy of **"Central Banks and World Markets - How to Detect Early Warning Signals of Financial Distress."**

This book will provide you with key high-level insights on how to detect early warning signals of systemic risk and financial distress with unconventional approaches, and more that every Investor, Chairman, Chief Executive Officer, Chief Investment Officer, Chief Risk Management Officer, Board Member needs today.

Let's get started with providing those insights to detect what is wrong at the system level in today's markets; detecting early signals of financial distress and systemic risk, and markets uncertainties; to enable better decision making on balance sheet priority risk detection and response right now.

Sincerely,

Fernando Walter Lolo and Cathal Rabbitte

www.DirectionalAlpha.com

ABOUT THE AUTHORS

Fernando Walter Lolo and Cathal Rabbitte specialize in systemic risk, financial modeling, investments, balance sheet hedging, and fiduciary duty at www.DirectionalAlpha.com whose accomplishments include:

Fernando Walter Lolo

- Fernando Walter Lolo specializes in Alternative Investments and Global-Macro strategies. Fernando founded Directional Alpha as a private asset management fund focused exclusively on tail risk, volatility trading, and hedging. In 2017, Directional Alpha was re-launched as a knowledge-driven boutique, with a relentless forward looking focus on systemic risk and world-macro conditions.

- Fernando has 20+ years of global track record in finance. Fernando focuses his businesses on solid ground unconventional/unorthodox approaches, as part of a difficult built-up rethought process of traditional/conventional methods.

- Fernando focuses on volatility, tail risks, and world-macro financial events, and he was also an active angel investor only in high-impact selective deals. He has advised on international finance, FSB - Financial Stability Board, and G-20 high-profile related issues at the Ministry of Economy and Finance of Argentina. Prior to that, he worked in Global Alternative Investments for 10+ years at the World Bank Group in Washington, DC. Before that, he worked in Quantitative Finance, Corporate Finance, and Risk Management in Latin America (LATAM).

- Fernando refined his specializations at Ivy-leagues by focusing on Investments, Fundraising, Investor Psychology-Risk Profiles, Global-Macro & Prop Trading, and Geopolitical International Finance. Fernando holds an MBA, a Master in Finance, and Post-graduate Degrees in Financial Engineering & Quantitative Finance from Harvard University, Columbia University, Universidad Torcuato Di Tella, Universidad de Buenos Aires, and Johns Hopkins University. In addition, he is a Certified Public Accountant (Argentina) and holds the CAIA designation (Chartered Alternative Investment Analyst) from CAIA Association.

- During his career, Fernando worked in the US, Emerging Markets (LATAM), and Europe.

Cathal Rabbitte

- Cathal Rabbitte, FIA is an actuary, analyst, strategist, and journalist specializing in modeling coherence and the translation of developing macro economic themes into usable modeling insights and workable strategy.

- Cathal serves as external Contributing Editor at Directional Alpha. He has over 20 years of experience in Europe, Asia, and Africa, primarily in insurance and reinsurance.

- As a journalist, he has extensive archiving and research experience as well as broad and deep knowledge of historical trends with a strong ability to put risk into cultural and historical contexts and to help articulate the limits of financial modeling to detect signals of the future and to minimize risk given economic turbulence.

- Cathal has over 15 years of experience reporting and analyzing economic themes for various media. Cathal has analyzed and written extensively about corporate collapses and the near death of top global Reinsurance and Insurance Companies during the initial stage of the World Financial crisis in 2008-10. The key in those cases was incoherent modeling and poor corporate governance responses to shifting risk developments.

Work History:

- Before the 2008 crisis, both authors already foresaw that crisis coming while working at other organizations (World Bank Group and Swiss Re). They were exposed to market crises such as the Mexican "Tequila" crisis, Asian "Tigers" crisis, Brazil, Ecuador, Argentina crisis, Russian crisis, the dot-com crisis, geopolitical crisis, tail events such as 2008 crisis, and other events of high volatility such as China markets volatility events, Brexit, the 2016 US Elections, French Elections, and alike.

- The authors have developed complementary skills by mastering traditional methods, and then subsequently unconventional methods in finance, world macro economics, investments, markets, volatility, tail, and systemic risks.

- The authors focus on world-macro strategies and specialize in coherent high-level analysis aiming to avoid the group think of the market. Even before re-launching Directional Alpha in 2017, the authors have re-confirmed that financial markets continue to be heavily influenced by group think. This reality calls for a fresh view incorporating the fact that markets are not in business-as-usual any longer, and therefore, modeling needs to reflect this in order to protect fiduciary duty.

- The high-level insights in this book are not driven by what the markets are doing. The authors do not follow market trends, but we consider a mosaic view of the system, including fundamentals, technical, history, asset bubbles, debt, geopolitics, international relations, power considerations and investment finance.

- This book's core focus is on systemic and tail risks which are ignored by markets and not reflected in market pricing. The authors look at structural reasons behind developments, and also why prior events happen. They understand the key difference between cyclical and systematic crises.

- They have strong communications skills and deep market knowledge concerning events over the last 30 years. Both authors understand many weaknesses in modeling and investments given that very few models take a systematic world approach as they do, as they instead mostly follow market pricing views. They are interested in what is happening and not in what people think is happening. After a long walk, they re-created Directional Alpha - World-Macro.

Personal Information:

- The authors come from different backgrounds, having complimentary skillsets, and a mix of insurance-macro and hedge fund global-macro investment skills.
- Given their worldwide experience, it was to be expected that we might have different views and angles about politics, current affairs, and so on; however, we believe that our diverse backgrounds and experience foster respect, integrity, humility, and further, to focus on discussing the best solutions to any topic by focusing on What is right, rather than Who of us is right. We consider this is one of our great Assets. Our focus is on risk and opportunity.
- Both authors have a solid experience over a wide range of geographies (US, EU, Latin America, Asia,

Middle East, and Eastern Europe). Their understanding of cultures, doing businesses, finance, investments, and politics across many languages is high level.

- They have extensive experience in world macro issues such as financial crises, tail risks, modeling weaknesses, G-20, Financial Stability Board - FSB issues, Insurance & Financial Regulations, Pensions, Hedge Funds, Asset Management, Alternative Investments, Regulations (e.g. Solvency 2, Basel III), Investment Management, Fundraising, Investor Psychology, Trading, Corporate Finance, Journalism, and Risk Management.

- In a nutshell, they have developed a thorough understanding of the underlying drivers of world macro events. As a result, we are driven to demystify often complex subjects into the form of accessible analytics, with a focus on coherent problem-solving approaches.

DEDICATION

To our Kids: Benjamin, Tim, and Éadaoin.

To our Families, Corinne, Friends, Colleagues, and Readers, past, present, and future.-

In memory of Jean Francois Perroud
And Jorge Walter Lolo.

ACKNOWLEDGEMENTS

Thanks to all who accompanied us on this long journey, which was *a long Walk*.

www.DirectionalAlpha.com

INTRODUCTION

This book addresses critical issues of **how Central Banks have been operating since 2008 and how markets are still being influenced by their decisions. It provides unconventional approaches to detect early warnings and signals of systemic risks and financial distress**. It will provide you with **high-level insights** on **how to read both Central Banks decisions and Markets' reactions**. It is designed to *examine the specific fundamentals of systemic risks when Markets embrace in an incomplete reading of Central Banks operations* at the system level, **which many times are disregarded by financial markets and conventional thinking**.

This book **focuses on key areas of risk such as interest rates, bond yields, inflation, deflation, reflation, economic growth drivers under different conventional and unconventional economic theories, assets, gold, pricing, core challenges of interest rates decisions, and how Central Banks influence models and Market Participants actions at the global level**. Further, it

provides coherent assessments that *every Investor, Chairman, Chief Executive Officer, Chief Investment Officer, Chief Risk Management Officer, Board Member* **needs to know to hedge their investment decisions in order to fulfill the fiduciary duty.**

Since many models provide incomplete data; mistakes happen especially if early signals of financial distress are not captured by them. This book provides coherent analyses to help reduce those mistakes that most often cause **Investors, Chairmen, CEOs, CIOs, CROs, and Board Members** to *fail completely* with these issues and **what information they need to PRIORITIZE!**

These mistakes stop most of them dead in their tracks, really before they ever even get started. In summary, this book provides:

- High-level insights on how to understand *Central Banks' dynamics to detect early signals of systemic risk formation and financial distress.*

- Coherent assessments of *markets uncertainties specifically created by Central Banks' models.*

- Robust analyses for better decision making on *priority risks to improve hedging and investment decisions.*

- Assessments of *herd mentality in current markets and groupthink dynamics to support suitable alternative reallocation decisions.*

www.DirectionalAlpha.com

Fernando Walter Lolo and Cathal Rabbitte are specialists on the subject of World-Macro and are sharing their extensive knowledge and experience to help People avoid the most damaging mistakes in this area so every **Investor, Chairman, CEO, CIO, CRO, Board Member** can better understand **how Central Banks influence world markets by knowing how to detect early signals of financial distress.**

So, let's just jump right in.

WHAT IS GROUPTHINK AND MARKET PSYCHOLOGY?

"The biggest risk in the financial system is psychological."

We **define groupthink as a process that involves all market participants** who **dynamically** act, react, think, and pause in unison as a herd by **basing their actions on all types of shared knowledge and by prioritizing them within the scope of the average boundaries of a common thinking with different behavioral decision biases.** As such, groupthink is **a dynamic compact that labels contrarian to the average or outliers to those ideas, thoughts, or actions that are rare or labeled as difficult to happen, which indeed are not within the crowd direction.** This process may have had been labeled in the past as market psychology or herd mentality; however, these later are static characteristics. **Groupthink is dynamic, and perhaps, a silent process that can last decades or more.** Further, **it usually adds to both extremes; systemic risks as well as large positive opportunities. Again, we find that one key differentiation factor is that **groupthink is indeed a dynamic compact, which can behave randomly, especially during fragmented or rare extreme events.** In parallel, **denial is usually reinforced ex-ante by the avoidance of alternative options,** regardless whether they could be good or bad, but **many times that denial responds to** biases and psychological patterns of **fear.**

INTEREST RATES, CENTRAL BANKS, BONDS, YIELDS, BALANCE SHEETS

"... *a random talk:*

Joe: How much is our exposure?

Bill: A pile of money.

Joe: If I ask you 'how much,' your reply should be a number, right? Again, how much Bill?

Bill: A substantial amount Joe."

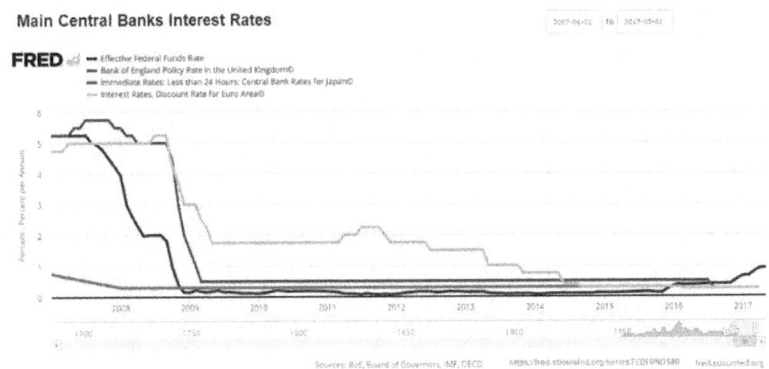

In most Organization for Economic Co-operation and Development (OECD) countries, interest rates and bond yields have never been as low as they are now. The theory behind Quantitative Easing (QE) programs are backed by the idea that inflation is a function of money supply. The four main global Central Banks, namely the Federal Reserve (FED), the European Central Bank (ECB), and the Bank of England (BoE), and the Bank of Japan (BoJ) have expanded their balance sheets to the tune of approximately USD 14 Trillion. Since inception, these initiatives' objectives tried to drive economic growth and inflation.

However, it was observed that during this long period of QE programs, they fed a high assets price increase of approximately USD 35 trillion. The results of the original objectives of the QE initiatives are yet to be seen. Furthermore, they are yet to be retrospectively evaluated.

Some questions remain, especially on where the money ended up. In simple terms, questions are starting to emerge on whether the money was channeled into production and industry, or poured into equities and credit of all shapes and sizes; as well as, what were the proportions and levels of funding into each destination.

This leads to consider the impact on the time value of money. As a reference, Irish bonds were yielding 13% a few years ago. Today investors get less than 100 basis points. Even Greek yields are lower than 6%. Junk bonds can be found with yields as low as 4%. Sovereign bonds worth over USD 10 Trillion have negative yields. The notion of the time value of money is in bad health.

Part of the situation can be explained by how markets work. If Central Banks want to buy assets, markets will oblige. However, markets mostly operate as herds and follow trends. An Investor might buy a junk bond yielding 6% with no intention of holding it to maturity. If that Investor thinks yields will go lower with the trend, s/he will hold on and offload at 4%. This leads to another observation on Balance sheets. They were troubled in late 2008 and 2009, but now they have a look of health thanks to asset reflation. Trends can suddenly reverse. The period following the 2008 crisis was marked by the unwinding of market pricing excesses. Bond Yields adjusted to a new reality. Market trends can be offloaded when the facts change.

The generalized fall in yields has driven important structural changes in financial markets. Pension funds and Insurance companies have been driven in large part out of their traditional sovereign bond holdings and forced by yield considerations into Corporate Bonds and Junk Bonds. These two asset classes have attractive yields, but they come with unpriced levels of tail risk. Economic history evidence is that Corporate Bonds tend to experience liquidity issues in a crisis, for example.

Along all these years, the effects of Central Banks' programs have led to higher equity prices in many markets. Further, a deeper look can assume with a high degree of confidence that these initiatives sustained for a long period have been the main factor driving equity prices. However, a parallel analysis should be considered when observing Revenue growth, which has been low.

Junk bonds require strong revenue growth to justify valuations on an ongoing basis. If junk bonds are revealed to be overpriced, so too will other bonds. If sustainable economic growth during this long period cannot be justified with strong factual evidence, it is hard to see bond prices being justified over the medium term. Liquidity can be compromised. Any bond revaluation will have balance sheet consequences.

Another impact was on Volatility, which was artificially suppressed even while structural risk has remained elevated. Factual evidence of sustainable economic growth during this long period of relative quiet is very thin on the ground.

In essence, the emergence of negative and very low yield bonds in recent years is highly significant since it implies that investors rate factors other than a return on investment as more important. The time value of money is suspended as is the most fundamental principle of corporate finance, that risk is rewarded with a return. Negative yield debt demonstrates that there are practical limits as to how much debt can be added to the financial system in the absence of sustainable economic growth.

The flip side of ever lower debt yields is ever higher debt prices since price moves inversely to yield. This is the name of the game in 2017. This could be recognized as debt deflation. Some outcomes are: companies are run as bonds, debt replaces equity, and buybacks take preference over investment. Therefore, there is no growth exit from this state since excess debt generates deflation. Deflation is not a plausible medium-term state since it reduces debt sustainability and also increases political implications.

Debt has at least two natural implications. These are inflation and politics. If growth is subordinated to the interests of debt, debt eventually becomes a political issue. Investors should beware of the normalization of deviance. That state of diverging from normally accepted standards, such as negative yield bonds for a long period, may indicate elevated levels of systemic risk, especially if the system finds difficulties to iterate itself back to equilibrium.

Systemic risk levels are high. Coherent fact-based analysis, effective coordination, and suitable timely actions are required.

REFLATION, CHALLENGES, OPPORTUNITIES, AND EXPECTATIONS

Two weeks before the US presidential election, asset managers were counseling investors to stick with bonds that were going to offer steady returns under the watchful eye of the Federal Reserve (FED), given the likelihood of a business-as-usual win for Hillary Clinton.

The market did not expect a Donald Trump win. Markets have not been effective at predicting political events. The world's biggest hedge fund estimated a 10.4% fall in equities if Trump won. Another big global bank thought the S&P500 would fall 15%.

Trump's victory and the manner of his acceptance speech sent the market off on a wave of positivity. Some themes appeared to predominate the political landscapes following the election:

- A USD 1 Trillion investment program focusing on infrastructure.

- The money would be funded by debt and public-private partnerships.

- Trump would focus on fiscal and monetary rather than solely monetary policy.

- The FED would be reshaped.

- Regulation concerning finance and healthcare would be changed.

- Protection of American jobs is a priority.

- Corporate taxes would be cut to 20% or lower.

- Sectoral budget spending increases facing trade-offs.

Some early assumptions were drawn by the market:

- Financials should rise in value as the economy reflates and drives interest rates higher, to the benefit of net interest income and investment earnings.
- Technology stocks with their exposure to Asian supply chains are vulnerable to the imposition of any trade mechanisms.
- Any anti-trust style action against monopolies will hurt tech stocks.
- Healthcare and pharma sticks will benefit from changes to healthcare regulation.
- Prison sticks are more attractive as are big industrial stocks, such as Caterpillar, that stand to benefit from infrastructure investment.

- Stocks which mirror bonds, such as utilities, have less upside in a reflationary scenario.
- The dollar will benefit from reflation as higher interest rates attract money from emerging markets.
- Bonds subsequently fell in value as a reflection of fears around a move away from monetary policy. Fiscal activity will be funded by an estimated USD 7.2 Trillion in new debt over ten years. This would increase the supply of debt without supporting debt demand and has this led to a fall in prices equivalent to a rise in yields of 0.5% in the ten years bond since the election.

Markets tend to react before outcomes are visible. This is because markets operate in herds and need clear guidance on where they are going the minute change in direction is obvious. Markets focus on momentum rather than structural issues. Many investment houses have linked Trump as the second coming of Reagan.

A feature of the Trump win is the fact that markets and the world expected him to lose. Further, the result was such a surprise that the market herd started to the downside early on the following day and then reverted to positive territory at the end of the session. The range between -1% and +1% was traveled in a matter of hours. After the second day post-election, markets continued with their optimism after reversal from downward moves during the pre-market hours of the post-election day. Detaching from the election analysis, this demonstrates that markets tend to operate groupthink, behaving in herds regardless of the outcome or any fundamentals.

In 2017, Quarter 1 bond prices have recovered. The US Dollar fell for seven straight months. It became clear that markets run in groupthink.

Some challenges were already gathering momentum:

- The Republican Congress has to approve any increases in debt that were already increased and inherited from the previous administration. This was one of the key drivers of political gridlock when the debt ceiling had to be raised. It is estimated that the inherited debt totaled USD 20 Trillion as of April 2017. US corporates are already overloaded with debt after at least USD 2 Trillion worth of buybacks over the last four years. It is worth noting that a typical Standard and Poors 500 balance sheet is not ready for reflation yet.
- The new administration needs to tread carefully with China, who is a key owner of US Treasuries.
- Voters will expect anti-trust actions against monopolies. The tech sector seems quite vulnerable, and implementation of this measure should be carried out carefully considering difficult tradeoffs.
- A focus on growth and job creation is underway along with a new definition of trade, message that was delivered at the G-20 meetings in Germany.
- It is worth noting, that currently the US economy suffers from low productivity growth, and is in a low-interest rate environment.
- The political landscape is becoming challenging (e.g., healthcare reform, others).

A combination of a dynamic fiscal and monetary policies may be considered to support demand for growth. A strong US Dollar will cut into corporate profits while noting that approximately 40% of Standard and Poors 500's earnings are generated abroad. Coordination and effective dynamic policy actions will be key drivers to growth and job creation, but noting the USD 20 Trillion debt inherited challenge.

WHY PAYRISES ARE IMPORTANT IN THE GENERATION OF ECONOMIC GROWTH

The US economy has been growing more slowly than during the 30 year period following World War II. Economists have tended to explain poor growth using a slowdown in business productivity. But even after productivity growth returned in the mid-1990s, average wages continued to with low growth. Economic expansion in the current economic system is commonly attributed to debt issuance and globalization. Both low wage growth and high corporate profits play a big role.

Earnings for the 500 largest companies in the Standard & Poors Index have recently risen to record levels on the back of very low interest rates, financial engineering, low wages, and layoffs. They have not grown on the back of revenue growth. In fact, revenues have not grown in line with earnings. This is an early signal for future earnings growth. Revenues depend on the ability of the consumer to pay prices demanded. Without payrises, this capacity is reduced. There is only so much lifting that financial engineering can manage.

As a reference, economists try to understand business cycles. We found the following definition interesting: *"Business cycles consist of recurring alternations of expansion and contraction in aggregate economic activity....The economy seems to be incapable of remaining on an even keel, and periods of expanding activity always and all too soon give way to declining production and employment. Further, and this is the essence of the problem, each upswing or downswing is self-reinforcing. It feeds on itself and creates further movement in the same direction; once begun, it persists in a given direction until forces accumulate to reverse the direction."* Source: Robert A. Gordon, Business Fluctuations, New York, 1952, p. 214.

Given all these, macroeconomics today is in a state of an ideological flux. "If deflation is good for my pension, is it good for me? Who shall be happy?" Economic growth without wage growth is by definition limited since corporate revenues ultimately depend on the spending of consumers. A catch-22 situation?

On a worldwide basis, Quantitative Easing (QE) programs were designed to jump start the world economy by reducing the cost of credit. In 2014, Merrill Lynch calculated that that global central banks boosted liquidity by roughly USD 9 Trillion since equities bottomed in 2009. Over the same period, world markets capitalization rose USD 35 Trillion while the world economy expanded only by USD 14 Trillion.

The level of unemployment in an economy may give a different angle to the payrise issue. For example, the UK has lower unemployment than France. For France, new jobs are more important than payrises, although sustainable growth will require both. In the case of the UK, the lack of payrises between 2011 and 2015 means that the Government could not meet its deficit targets, perhaps one of the reasons the population chose to leave the European Union via a referendum.

The following chart shows how benefits paid to employees have been reducing – employer funded healthcare in the US:

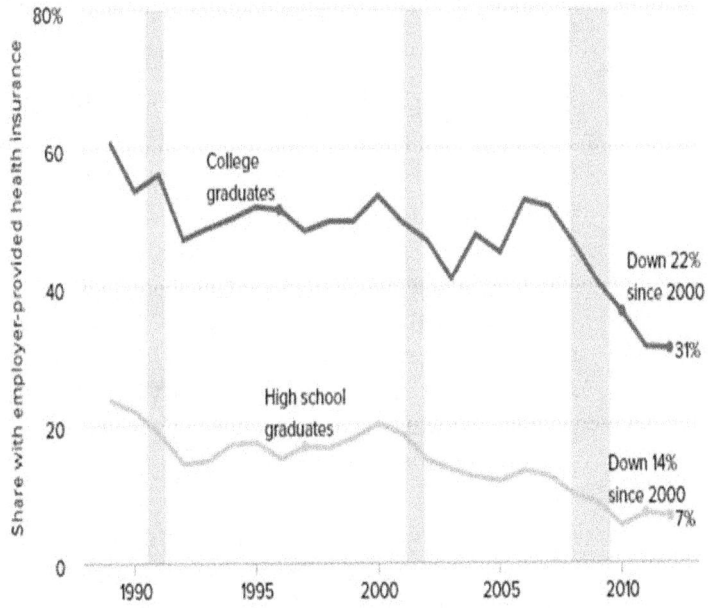

Source: Economic Policy Institute, 6 January 2016.

In some American companies, health insurance price increases absorb the funds that would otherwise be available to generate payrises. There are many influences on low to stagnant pay rises.

Joseph Schumpeter noted that history is a record of effects that nobody intended to create. Linking this concept with today's situation, we can summarize the following:

- Across the Organization for Economic Co-operation and Development (OECD) countries, wages continue to increase slowly.

- In order to get the US or Eurozone economy back to equilibrium and to yield back to a healthy 4% return, the economy requires strong job creation, sustainable payrises, and bank lending at a higher level to allow the authorities to tighten policy.

- Loan take up recently has been low. In the two months that ended in January 2017, US banks reduced total lending. People do not appear to be interested in debt.

- Even though corporate earnings in Europe and the US have been growing over the last 18 months, revenues have not been. This is linked to low payrises and low wages. Without revenue growth, companies are unlikely to meet profit growth expectations.

- Coordination between countries could help, but which approaches will prevail in today's geopolitical map?

Current approaches are more likely to be tested, as are the trade-off assessments to bring the system back to equilibrium. Each upswing or downswing is self-reinforcing. At the corporate level, how many Chief Financial Officers (CFO) or Shareholders are likely to see the benefit of a companywide payrise? How many analysts care about the trend in earnings? As J.K. Galbraith wrote in a spirit of grim reality when he noted that: "The conventional wisdom" gives way not so much to new ideas as to "the massive onslaught of circumstances with which it cannot contend."

As history reminds us, too many years of the same things generate consequential path dependent outcomes. This applies to interest rates, inflation, growth rates, and indeed, too long periods of low payrises. **Dealing with the results of ex-ante trade-off decisions are carried over to a later stage, where eventually the consequences may become unmanageable if not addressed in time.**

WHY THE FEDERAL RESERVE (FED) HAS CONTINUALLY FACED CHALLENGES SINCE THE LEHMAN BROTHERS COLLAPSE

The Federal Reserve saved the US economy from a return to the conditions that drove the Great Depression of the 1930s by cutting interest rates sharply in the aftermath of the Lehman Brothers collapse in 2008. It has been less successful in guiding the US economy back to "exit velocity" since. Fed Chairman Ben Bernanke gave an important policy speech on March 2013 in which he outlined the Fed's understanding of medium term economic developments:

"If, as the FOMC anticipates, the economic recovery continues at a moderate pace, with unemployment slowly declining and inflation expectations remaining near 2 percent, then long-term interest rates would be expected to rise gradually toward more normal levels over the

next several years. This rise would occur as the market's view of the expected date at which the Federal Reserve will begin the removal of policy accommodation draws nearer and then as accommodation is removed. Some normalization of the term premium might also contribute to a rise in long-term rates." Source: Annual Monetary/Macroeconomics Conference: The Past and Future of Monetary Policy, sponsored by Federal Reserve Bank of San Francisco, San Francisco, California. March 1, 2013.

The first order issue is that it is 2017 and the Fed funds rate is 0.75 to 1.0% and not 3% as projected. Why is this then? A huge part of the reason is that the FED theory started to be delinked from the real economy. As Bernanke explained in his 2013 speech, the Fed has been following the same economic theory since 1979.

"As you know, under the leadership of Chairman Paul Volcker, the Federal Reserve in 1979 fundamentally changed its approach to the issue of ensuring price stability. This change involved an important rethinking on the part of policymakers. By the end of the 1970s, Federal Reserve officials increasingly accepted the view that inflation is a monetary phenomenon, at least in the medium and longer term." Source: ibid.

This was the work of Milton Friedman and others. M1 Money supply in the US was increased by 11% per annum between 2010 and 2015 without a corresponding increase in inflation. Money velocity remains very low. Quantitative Easing may have done the opposite of what the Fed intended because instead of driving growth it has delivered a very large bond bubble.

Bernanke outlined the importance of Fed inflation targeting in his 2013 speech:
"The anchoring of long-term inflation expectations near 2 percent has been a key factor influencing long-term interest rates over recent years. It almost certainly helped mitigate the strong disinflationary pressures immediately following the crisis. While I have not shown expected

inflation for other advanced economies, the pictures would be very similar- -again, except for Japan." Source: ibid.

Before that, Bernanke gave an important speech in January 2009 outlining the Fed's communication approach to markets.

"One important tool is policy communication. Even if the overnight rate is close to zero, the Committee should be able to influence longer-term interest rates by informing the public's expectations about the future course of monetary policy. To illustrate, in its statement after its December meeting, the Committee expressed the view that economic conditions are likely to warrant an unusually low federal funds rate for some time. To the extent that such statements cause the public to lengthen the horizon over which they expect short-term rates to be held at very low levels, they will exert downward pressure on longer-term rates, stimulating aggregate demand. It is important, however, that statements of this sort be expressed in conditional fashion--that is, that they link policy expectations to the evolving economic outlook. If the public were to perceive a statement about future policy to be unconditional, then long-term rates might fail to respond in the desired fashion should the economic outlook change materially." Source: Stamp Lecture, London School of Economics, London, England. January 13, 2009.

Communication is second order when the theory provides different outcomes than those expected.

The Fed must be surprised at the outcome three years after Bernanke's speech. There may, in fact, be a limit to how much debt can be loaded onto the real economy before deflation turns up.

The absence of growth and the appearance of signs of deflation in the US economy represent a challenge for the US financial sector. A majority of voters in 2016's presidential election can be read as a need for change to the economic status quo. The Federal Reserve is now expected to raise interest rates rapidly. However, pension schemes, endowments, banks, and insurers will face difficult decisions.

The Fed now needs to understand why Ben Bernanke's reflation plan differed from planned outcomes before endorsing any new plans, of which one area of concern is how the Fed models the US economy. In this regard, the Financial Times gave an overview recently as follows:

"The Atlanta Fed's GDP Now model estimates first-quarter GDP growth at just 0.3 per cent. This extends the long-running conundrum of punchy jobs growth combined with damp GDP data", Mr. Bullard said, adding his bank's model had repeatedly been indicating that 3 percent growth was *"just around the corner."* Source: Financial Times, April 17, 2016.

However, this was not happening. Markets did respond enthusiastically to the US election and yields did rise; subsequently, they fall again as groupthink intensified. There are still challenges in the real economy that are delinked from all time high levels of market prices, which coincide with predominantly stagnant revenues.

As a result, we come to the following key implications:

1. The new Administration needs to tread very carefully since it may be difficult to unwind the cumulative effects of 40 years of economic policy in one term.

2. It would be difficult to detect the drivers to generate inflation.

3. The most suitable balance sheet would appear to be one that recognizes the reality of deflation,

which manifests itself in lower sales, earnings, hiring, and growth.

4. Given the level of debt, it is at risk of write downs if deleveraging is accelerated.

5. A coordinated effort to align monetary policy with fiscal policy towards growth and job creation will become a priority under an unconventional joint effort.

CENTRAL BANKS, ASSETS, GOLD

"The question is not what you look at, but what you see." Henry D. Thoreau

"... AND #1: What you see will define what You Become.

... AND #2: What you Become will define what your Destiny is.

... AND #3: The Journey will help People to refine themselves with new alternatives to Grow and to Own their Destiny."

---

1) To date, the following 10 Central Banks concentrate USD22+ Trillion in Assets:

- US Federal Reserve
- European Central Bank

- Bank of Japan
- The People's Bank of China
- Swiss National Bank
- Bank of Russia
- Central Bank of Brazil
- Central Bank of the Kingdom of Saudi Arabia
- Bank of England
- Central Bank of India

- Of the USD22+ Trillion, around 76% are concentrated in China, the US, Japan, and the Eurozone.

- Central Banks increased their assets by 3.7 times since 2007.

- To date, these assets represent around 30% of World Total GDP and about 32% of the World Stock Markets Capitalization.

2. Top 30 Official Gold Holdings by Country/Organization as of July 2017 (in tonnes):

1. The United States   8,133.5
2. Germany   3,375.6
3. International Monetary Fund (IMF)   2,814.0
4. Italy   2,451.8
5. France   2,435.9
6. China   1,842.6
7. Russia   1,706.8
8. Switzerland   1,040.0
9. Japan   765.2

10. Netherlands   612.5
11. India   557.8
12. ECB   504.8
13. Turkey   441.3
14. Taiwan   423.6
15. Portugal   382.5
16. Saudi Arabia   322.9
17. The United Kingdom   310.3
18. Lebanon   286.8
19. Spain   281.6
20. Austria   280.0
21. Kazakhstan   275.4
22. Belgium   227.4
23. Philippines   196.3
24. Venezuela   187.5
25. Algeria   173.6
26. Thailand   152.4
27. Singapore   127.4
28. Sweden   125.7
29. South Africa   125.3
30. Mexico   120.2

- *Total World Reserves: 33,399.21 tonnes, of which the above first 15 countries' reserves total 27,487.9 tonnes (representing more than 82% of the total world reserves). Source: World Gold Council*

- *Price of Gold (Comex August 29, 2017): USD1,211.60*

THE REALITY OF DEFLATION IN THE EUROZONE AND ELSEWHERE

Most people and businesses operate in terms of business-as-usual (BAU). For most businesspeople, business as usual means growth: *"Next year's numbers will be bigger than this year's."* We are very susceptible to stability bias, given the groupthink belief that if there was growth in the past, then there will be growth in the future, regardless of what we do. This was the case in the past but will it work in the next few years?

The Euro was introduced in 1999. The institutional design most resembles the economic principles of the gold standard which gave rise to the economic crisis of the 1930s, which was a period of deflation. The principles of the Euro are that fiscal policy is ineffective; inflation is caused exclusively by money supply growth, and the real economy quickly and automatically returns to full employment in response to negative shocks.

Following the collapse of Lehman Brothers in 2008, economic policy makers in the Federal Reserve and other Central Banks were determined not to repeat the mistakes of the 1930s, when central banks waited too long to cut interest rates and allowed deflation to set in. In 2008, rate cuts were swift, but it has not been possible to restore interest rates to their previous level. One of the outcomes of this is that growth in the Eurozone has been low in the period since the Lehman Brothers collapse.

It is now nine years on, and there are increasing signs of deflation in the real economy, despite the best efforts of Central Banks. Across the Organization for Economic Co-operation and Development (OECD) countries, the money supply has increased by more than 5% a year without generating similar increases in inflation or aggregate demand. The money to inflation link is not behaving as it has in the past or as economic theory says it should. Signs of deflation proliferate across the OECD countries, although they are more pronounced in the Eurozone. A brief description of deflationary effects are summarized below:

- *Bond yields are very low.*

- *Retail companies such as Macys and Wal-Mart, or transportation companies such as Maersk, and FMCG outfits such as Nestle are facing slowing growth and falling margins.*

- *Companies prefer buybacks over investment, given the economic environment.*

- *Wage growth is lower than usual.*

So the question is what is deflation and what does it entail?

- Under deflation a pot of cash has an increased purchasing power over time, i.e., just leaving it there means that you can buy more with it in the future. This is the exact opposite of BAU since deflation for a long period deters growth. Under deflation, the following characteristics can be found:

- The time value of money is reversed. A dollar next year is worth more than a dollar now.

- Prices fall. As a reference, prices have been falling in Switzerland for five years, the result of an overvalued currency. Tourism suffers as tourists decide to holiday elsewhere. Jobs are lost as countries hit by deflation lose competitiveness.

- When prices are falling, nominal interest rates must be pushed to very low levels to boost output. Output stagnates since consumers do not have payrises (or, even worse, lose their jobs) to support higher prices. Unemployment becomes a structural issue. Insufficient new jobs are created. "Beggar my neighbor" policies in other countries generate currency wars which favor imports, threatening local jobs.

- Wages remain stagnant. Deflation does not create the well-paid jobs needed to boost growth. Certain investment professionals may attempt to point out that a stagnant wage under deflation of 1% increases in real terms.

- Quantitative Easing (QE) programs are designed to generate growth, but under deflation, they become less effective. The money QE produces is not invested in growth, but instead, indirectly feeds into asset bubbles. Consumers are not tempted to borrow money to start businesses. The velocity of money is very low.

- Investment Banking struggles. Certain banks have difficulty covering their cost of capital.

- Money is invested in companies that operate like bonds and return as much cash as possible to investors, either via dividends or share buybacks. Companies are not encouraged to invest in growth, new hires, or staff development. Lower growth becomes a result of deflation processes given that the logic is focused on taking cash out of companies.

- Stocks, which are high because of buybacks rather than sustainable increases in profit, are more than likely overvalued.

- The logic of deflation derails investing in business growth or giving people payrises since it is not rewarded by the market. Deflation is essentially about capital protection by investors, given that it does not produce high growth as theory expects.

- The lack of payrises feeds through to falling revenues that entail lower growth and employment, which are visible across the economy.

Conclusions regarding deflation follow:

Adjusting BAU balance sheets becomes critical. BAU balance sheets become dangerous under deflation since fixed income instruments are overvalued. As a reference, bond sustainability requires growth and eventual bond price corrections result in cuts to shareholder equity. The safest balance sheets under deflation are those who hold no bonds and the safest markets under deflation are those with lower levels of debt.

It is suitable to check the actions of countries facing deflation, especially which combinations of economic policies are undertaken given the constraints posed by deflation. This is particularly true given the difficulty and challenges represented in unwinding the cumulative effects across years of economic policies. Countries like those of the Eurozone will need to start considering reforms if they are to hedge themselves from the consequences of deflation.

CAN THE FEDERAL RESERVE (FED) RAISE INTEREST RATES FURTHER?

"(Random) Question: In the central bank's normalization processes component (2) Re: assets reduction; who will be the other side of the trade (a.k.a. Buyers). How will those potential Buyers value those assets 12 months after their purchases?"

The 2008 crisis that followed Lehman Brothers came as a surprise to everyone, and the Federal Reserve had to slash rates to zero to deal with that shock.

Alan Greenspan revealed in a subsequent interview that he thought C-Suite members would act in their fiduciary interest and understand tail risk.

By 2013, it was time to take stock. The FED's job is price stability, not hand-holding financial markets. At a 4% return,

Investment Banks can make profits by being themselves, pension funds are fundable, and banks make good net interest income. On March 1, 2013, Ben Bernanke, who replaced Greenspan at the FED, gave a very important speech in which he laid out a path that the US economy would be following over the next few years in order to get interest rates back to "normal," which meant 4%. Based on his speech, the market developed expectations of increasing interest rates from zero to 4%. Given this, the market took the advice on board and drove the dollar up by 20%. Lots of Asian and European money poured in given that higher rates mean attractive yields and markets had been starved of yield.

In 1980, the US financial market was valued at around 100% of GDP. By 2006, it had risen to 350%, a big increase since 1980. The financial sector extracts yield from the real economy in the form of interest, property rents, etc. A financial sector that is 3.5 times bigger than what the economy produces in a year needs to sustain itself with a lot of the value produced every year. Therefore, interest rates are key to the evolution of the financial sector. The lower rates go, the higher the present value of finance cash flow, and the higher the value of financial assets, and the bigger financial sector balance sheets.

Since 2008, financial sector money has flowed into every sector of the economy in the search for yield. There are competing claims on the money. So when the financial sector rises to 350% of GDP, it becomes hungry for higher yields at the expense of payrises.
After the Lehman Brothers collapse in 2008, asset values collapsed. Central Banks had trade-offs: they could either write down debt and start the economy off again on a stable footing, or they could re-inflate the economy in the hope that it would deliver sustainable economic growth but at the risk of another bubble. They chose the latter.

At 350% of GDP, interest rates cannot be very high. A rate of 5% would eat 17.5% of total economic activity every year. At 350% there are not enough quality assets. Money flows into poor credit, low-quality loans, and other risky assets.

In recent years, US unemployment has looked low, but only because the models ignore the labor participation rate. The US produced 14 million jobs during the last administration, of which most of the jobs were lower paying jobs. Given all these, there are tensions between debt levels and payrises with such a large financial sector.

As the famous saying goes, there is no such thing as a free lunch. Capital has the first call on the money. Capital benefits to the detriment of the real economy. So far, the FED has achieved low unemployment but low wage inflation. The result is visible given outcomes and rates that did not follow original Bernanke's expected path. This along with the fact that there have only been three rate rises since that Bernanke speech put more pressure on the FED actions on interest rates.

One key aspect of where we are now is that many Central Bank models struggle to factor in what is happening in the economy. For instance, the Atlanta FED's GDPnow model continues to predict a 3% GDP growth rate. Central Banks have full faith in their models that interpret that debt is risk-free. Notwithstanding, this pattern evidences live and difficult groupthink symptoms. One of the main reasons Central Banks had problems with their projections is simply because it does not include model debt, its level, and the effects of asset bubbles. In the fourth quarter of 2016, the growth rate was at 1.9%, lower than expected, reflecting the modeling conundrum and model challenge.

It is now 2017; the new Administration is facing a USD 20 Trillion debt economic problems with low interest rates, the employment issues mentioned earlier, and US consumption that still struggles to grow.

In addition to these, last year share buybacks took USD 1 Trillion out of Standard & Poors 500's balance sheets. That money could have been invested, but instead, it was paid to shareholders. There is no shortage of capital in the US now, and US banks have been cutting back on lending recently.

The reflation idea drove the markets from the summer of 2016 to the first quarter of 2017. Momentum was positive to date, but many questions remain open, some of which are listed below:

- *Is the amount of debt in the economy too large?*

- *How dependable are signs of activity such as purchasing managers indices that have consistently lost momentum since 2009?*

- *How dependable are asset prices as a guide to the future, since they often indicate that market expectations run too high; a notable feature of markets since 2009.*

- *Can the US generate enough payrises to power aggregate demand, consumption, and growth vis-à-vis the high level of corporate profits?*

- *Can the corporate sector act in its self interest to support aggregate demand, the key influence on corporate revenues?*

- *Given these, the question remains whether the FED can raise interest rates further.*

THE EURO AND ITS ONGOING CHALLENGES

In this piece, the ongoing challenges the Euro is still facing are analyzed. The analysis is structured in three sections as follows:

1. Is the Eurozone a monetary union?

2. What are the principles that underpin the Euro?

3. Which reforms would bring the Eurozone (EZ) out of the crisis zone?

Analyses follow:

1. Is the Eurozone a monetary union?

The Eurozone is often described as a monetary union. But what does it entail?
Since 2008, the Eurozone crisis has featured selective bank closures, the reintroduction of exchange controls and country

specific bailouts in the absence of a centralized bank recapitalization fund. When the German Herstatt Bank collapsed in Cologne in 1974, there was no closure of bank branches in its state of Nordrhein Westfalen nor were exchange controls introduced by the state authorities. Interest rates in Nordrhein Westfalen did not detach from rates elsewhere in Germany, nor did bank deposits flee the state. Germany can be considered as a monetary union. In 1984, during the time of the US bank failure, the state of Illinois was not expected to handle the fall-out. The US features monetary union characteristics such as federal responsibility for bank supervision, bank resolution, and the protection of bank creditors.

Due to political reasons, the Eurozone was established in 1999 as no more than a common currency area, with a Central Bank responsible only for monetary policy in the aggregate, in pursuit of an inflation target. There are significant differences between a common currency area and a monetary union. If the Eurozone were a monetary union, the history of the economic crisis and the recent history of the Swiss Franc would have been very different.

The Eurozone was established without any of the infrastructure distinguishing a monetary union from a simple common currency area. The key differences are:

- *A Banking union with a single supervisor.*
- *A single resolution authority.*
- *A common safety net involving.*
- *Deposit insurance.*
- *Fiscal backstops.*

- *Burden sharing.*

- *A credible Lender of Last Resort.*

2. What are the principles that underpin the Euro?

The Euro was devised just two years before the crash of 2001. By 1999, money seemed capable of generating more money at no risk. People in Europe subscribed to telecom IPOs that were sure to generate fortunes. The principles of the Euro were set in stone. These were as follow:

- *Fiscal policy is ineffective.*

- *Inflation is solely a function of the money supply.*

- *The economy responds quickly to external shocks, and unemployment is quickly rectified.*

In the Eurozone prior to the Lehman Brothers collapse, the interbank market functioned but with big capital flows as side effects, mostly from the north (banks) to south (Portugal, Italy, Ireland, Greece, and Spain - PIIGS). Pro-cyclicality was injected into the monetary transmission mechanism, and there was no possibility of controlling local interest rates. National bank regulators controlled their patches and cross border effects were ignored. When the 2008 crisis materialized, this impacted in Europe shortly after. The PIIGS were in trouble by 2009. The issue was debt, specifically bank debt. Lent by northern creditors to peripheral debtors. Financial regulations evidenced that politics and resources must go hand in hand.

3. Which reforms would bring the Eurozone out of the crisis zone?

Some of the principles to have a Eurozone with regulations suitable to today's markets' needs are the following:

- A banking union with the supervision of all Eurozone banks would limit the scope for regulatory arbitrage.

- Consistent application of prudent norms would help with the promotion of financial services in the single market. Since 2008, it can be evidenced that all the efforts have focused on monetary policy.

- Joint inspections, peer reviews, and cross country teams led by the European Central Bank (ECB) head are required. Incentives framework must be adapted to this.

- The Fortis and Dexia rescue in 2008 was cumbersome, especially with the cross border angles. A staffed and resourced regulatory system would over time build up expertise, and Europe could move away from the current *ad hoc* late-night-panic-driven response that has typified the crisis to date.

- If a bank becomes unviable and is non-systemic, it should be resolved at least cost.

- Where fiscal space is limited, then the European Stability Mechanism (ESM) should step in so that banks in trouble would have an owner of unquestioned strength. The ESM could help to stabilize prices but would not make expected losses - rather it would aim for what a patient investor would expect over time. Capital would not be injected into non-viable banks.

- The key problem currently can be said to be political in nature. Germany and other northern countries are unwilling to back the ESM with sufficient capital to work.

- Regarding resolution, a hierarchy of claims must be defined in order to reduce uncertainty around the capital structure.

- Insured depositors are given clear preference in legislation. The system would be pre-funded through risk based premiums, but in times of crisis, there might be a need for the involvement of the ECB, as a rapid Lender of Last Resort.

- The key challenge is to break the sovereign/bank link.

- The Cyprus crisis in 2012 was an example of a situation precisely where a banking union would have been preferable to the *ad hoc* method actually applied. A least cost method could have been used with either a good bank/bad bank or direct ESM recapitalization, the response could have been faster, and it would not have had to be dependent on the national system.

Meanwhile, on the monetary front, Quantitative Easing (QE) programs have still not delivered the originally expected outcomes. The target of the ECB is 2% inflation. It does not directly concern itself with unemployment. The combined effect of low growth, missing inflation targets, and the continued debt issuance is a reduction in debt sustainability, and a move in the direction of instability is plausible.

Therefore, many of the key principles of the system have still not delivered the originally expected outcomes, given the low inflation levels and the continued crisis upswings events, like Greece in 2017. Without reform to the Euro with infrastructure suitable to today's needs, involving bank recap, deposit insurance, and the like, the Eurozone itself will more than likely be challenged by the vast majority of average Eurozone citizens, who are still awaiting the outcomes of the policies designed a long time ago and during a period of relative economic calm. The waters will be tested again if volatility returns, but with a different geopolitical landscape and perhaps a more polarized audience.

WHAT IS WRONG AT THE SYSTEM LEVEL?

"... Loss of control is asymmetric. "

What is wrong at the system level and why we should expect more bankruptcies in a few years' time.

Take any 20-year yield curve. In most cases, rates at the short end are low, on either side of zero. Rates then move gradually upwards. This is the wisdom of the market. But is there any logic to it? **Why are rates low in the first place? Is this likely to continue? Or is it more likely to be reversed?**

Gradually rising rates are a sign of faith in business-as-usual, of a return to normality, but, **we are not in business-as-usual.**

Why are we still depending on Central Banks a decade after the outbreak of the crisis? Why do markets parse every word of Central Bankers? Can we get out of this crisis with or without them? Furthermore, how do we know we are in a crisis?

Central Banks target 2% inflation and have not been able to deliver this target since 2008. As a reference, the FED delivered 2% inflation in 5 months between 2008 and 2017. Interest rates are very low. **The velocity of money is near historic lows. Investment levels are very subdued.**

Even though unemployment seems to be good, wage inflation is not following the Philips curve. Poor wage inflation feeds into poor corporate revenues. The 50 largest Fast Moving Consumer Goods companies had falling sales in 2016; the latest elements of a decreasing pattern since 2011. Pepsi, Nestle, and Procter & Gamble core consumer goods sales are not growing enough. **This is not good.**

What are the key drivers of the crisis a.k.a "a managed depression"?

1. Low Interest **rates (maintained for a long period)**.
2. **Excessive debt levels.**
3. Lack of support for demand.
4. Income and wealth inequality.
5. Treatment of workers.
6. Corporate behavior.
7. **Polarization in societies.**
8. Geopolitical tensions.

1. Low Interest *rates*

The long term average is around 4% for example in Europe. Such a level of rates would allow banks to make money on lending, insurance companies to function, make pensions affordable and **restore the time value of money that is suspended at the moment, given a long period of ultra-**low interest **rates.**

Why are rates still so low?

As factual information, the money supply is greater than the capacity of the global economy to absorb it. The theory behind **Quantitative Easing (QE) programs was inspired by Milton Friedman, who understood that every time the money supply is increased, inflation follows.** He believed that growth was also a function of money supply.

Why did not that happen this time?

Friedman ignored the distribution of wealth. Roughly USD 14 Trillion in QE did not make it into the real economy. It went into speculation, for the most part, driving a bubble of over USD 35 Trillion.

2. Excessive Debt levels

Since 2008 the quantum of corporate debt in the US has grown from USD 4 Trillion to USD 9 Trillion. Around USD 1 Trillion of new debt is issued every year. In the past, debt **was an agent of economic growth**, and that was fact-based for many years. **However now, it is becoming an agent of deflation.**

Given that, money created must earn a return to support the debt issued, and this entails competing in every area of the real economy as a claim on real cash flows. The net effect can be seen in non-life reinsurance for example, where margins have fallen from 14% to 2% in the space of two years. **Reinsurers are squeezed on two sides: a) by yield seeking new money on one side, and, b) by the stagnating demand that is the feature of a debt soaked economy on the other side.**

Given that Central Banks have been unable to generate inflation, **there are question marks over their models.**

3. Lack of support for demand

Our economic system differs in two key respects from the one which preceded it:

> *1. In the system, there are no limits on the quantity of debt.*
>
> *2. The system **focuses on keeping inflation low** rather than on boosting demand.*

Demand is closely correlated to corporate revenues and represents the buying power of the population. Supporting demand supports corporate revenues. **Demand can be boosted in a number of ways including** payrises **and investments in skills.**

Over more than 40 years, skills have been neglected. Jobs for highly skilled manual workers have almost disappeared from many Organization for Economic Co-operation and Development (OECD) countries. It was observed by the media that investors like "jobs light" investments. This has medium-term consequences since it is not demand-friendly. Neither is low pay. **It all feeds into the overall level of demand. Without sustainable growth in demand, there cannot be sustainable economic growth.**

Demand is now at crisis levels across the OECD countries. The news that **the top 50 global fast-moving consumer goods (FMCG) companies are unable to grow sales is a sign of a system that is in crisis.** It is worth noting that it has taken many years to get to the current situation. **This is not something that did not happen overnight. As such, it cannot be reversed overnight.**

4. Income and wealth inequality

The US equity market capitalization represents approximately 35% of the total world stock markets capitalization. Households in the richest population of the US hold over half of all investments. QE increased their wealth. Their trade-off decisions between a financial investment and a real economy investment were biased towards the former given these policies.

In 1995, companies invested USD 4 for every dollar returned to shareholders. Today the ratio is 2:1. This also favors those who hold these investments. This is just a continuation of a system that has been in place for much more than 20 years. The very rich have been increasing their share of US income consistently since then. **QE policies boosted the value of financial assets, including bonds, thereby lowering the yield on bonds. Given these policies, very little of the USD 14 Trillion was invested in the real economy.**

Without investment in the real economy first, growth suffers. Without growth, deflation takes hold. With deflation, it is not possible to raise rates. A key reason for this is the quantum of debt that drives deflation. In effect, there is too much debt for rate rises. This is close to instability.

5. Treatment of Workers

In the US, wages have not kept pace with productivity since the mid-1970s. Over the long term, this has a huge cost. Wages as a percentage of corporate revenues fell from 66% in 1992 to 62% in 2000.

Ten years ago workers could expect regular payrises and a pension on retirement. In many sectors of the OECD countries, payrises are now a thing of the past. Over five years, this can amount to a sizeable sum which is not available to demand.

Weak unions are a key element of weak demand. If workers cannot negotiate payrises, demand suffers. In recent years listed companies have, despite stagnant revenues, boosted earnings via a combination of wage repression, financial engineering, tax cuts, cuts to investment, and low interest rates. When wage repression becomes systematic and operates over a period of years, **capital is preferred at the expense of demand; therefore, demand is weakened.**

When investment is cut, workers suffer since investment is a proxy for better experience leading to payrises. As an observation, Defined Benefit Pensions have become rare as the costs of retirement are passed on to individuals in the form of defined contribution pensions. This trend is very much part of the beliefs that motivate the actions of the members of societies to date. **However, as demand is low, GDP, Income, and Wealth cannot grow much further.**

6. The behavior of the corporate sector

Companies could make a yield of 5% on sovereign bonds before the 2008 crisis. They gave solid returns and have excellent liquidity. Quantitative Easing policies subsequently increased the monetary base and increased the price of most financial assets including bonds. **Many companies were forced out of majority sovereign bond holdings and into corporate bonds, which offer reasonable returns but poor liquidity. These assets are far riskier than sovereign bonds.**

For many companies, there is no escape. At the level of quoted companies, pressure from investors for dividends and buybacks is intense. Many companies are in effect run as bonds, with a cash focus. Some Reinsurers have paid out over USD15 Billion to shareholders since 2012, a period during which its revenues have been stagnant. Other large retailers have responded to competition by cutting the number of products, competing aggressively on price and reducing wage costs. The global paints industry has responded to stagnation with a wave of mergers and acquisitions, all involving large jobs cuts. **Consumer goods companies have problems with stagnant sales and with plans to cut annual spending.**

Given that companies are judged on metrics such as earnings per share, these type of metrics ignore investments. One view of today's corporate sector is that companies are being mined for cash. **Ratios like Sales as a percentage of Debt can provide an additional unconventional metric to assess corporate health.** However, QE policies maintained for a long period have affected these metrics. **Current realities differ from the originally planned effectiveness of QE policies.**

Historic parallels

If we take 1979-2017 and compare with 1870 to 1913, the following insights can be drawn. In the following 15 years, money became all powerful while reform languished. The fourth decade saw the development of popular resentment of money politics along with the growing monopoly power (Google, Amazon). **The political system now is marked by severe polarization which in essence means that nothing is done by the legislature.**

Why did not reflation work yet?

Reflation was the great hope of November 2016. It drove a strong rally in the US dollar, in US shares, and big falls in bond prices amidst hope that a combination of fiscal stimulus, infrastructure spending, and lighter regulation would spur corporate earnings and economic growth and lead to faster US interest rate rises.

In the US for instance, it did not happen yet. The cause is based on **the current system, which was neither upgraded nor designed for reflation. However, another important cause is that the polarization component has added volatility to new initiatives.** Even signs of split societies translate into uncertainties that lead companies to wait to invest. Investors want dividends and growth. Fiscal stimulus was a victim of polarization. It got held up behind many discussions in the US Congress and the Senate. Examples are Healthcare reform, another is Infrastructure spending, which has to be funded somehow. However, **it is worth noting** that similar facts and patterns with different angles have also been observed across the OECD countries.

7. Polarization in societies

Polarization brings uncertainties. Uncertainties add volatility. This is worsened given the current level of **groupthink**. These related components **can lead to a stage of "Pantano effect"** where nothing moves (or everything is put "on-hold").

8. Geopolitical tensions

If geopolitical tensions intensify further and diplomatic efforts are read as insufficient to reduce escalation, **then markets may read this as to an increased volatility and can cause systemic risk to materialize. Market groupthink plays a critical role during this stage, and cross-border coordination needs to happen rapidly** to level off market volatility.

The problem is not a lack of political focus. The problem is how the system has been designed. Aligned with that, supported models were designed to back a blaming system.

How did that model work in the past?

The key dynamics of the system are as follow:

1. *Every year more debt is added to the pile.*
2. *Corporate efforts are focused on investors rather than staff.*
3. *Investors prefer cash to revenue growth.*

4. Payrises *do not happen.*
5. *Demand continues to weaken.*
6. *Investment in the real economy continues to be ignored.*
7. *Corporate revenues do not grow.*
8. *The economic power of the richest segment of the population is reinforced via continued iterations of the above.*
9. *Economic growth turns lower as time passes.*
10. *Polarization is entrenched and problems fester.*
11. *Geopolitical tensions add more volatility to all of the above while challenging cross border coordination (in all aspects; including economic and trade).*

This has come for a change from a blaming system to an actionable ownership, empowerment, and accountability system

The system needs to change. The fast-moving consumer goods (FMCG) situation is a canary in the coal mine. There is a limit to the logic of current investment approaches. It brings these issues and incoherencies in the medium-term. Without investment in the real economy first, there can be no growth. **Without growth, debt can become both unmanageable and unsustainable.**

The system is moving in a particular direction that is not towards growth and stability.

What can we say about this?

Minsky's theorem of financial instability is a good place to start. One of the key assumptions is that there are financing systems which are stable and financing systems that are not stable. We currently have the latter. Minsky divides balance sheets into hedging units, speculative and Ponzi units. Hedging units can meet all of their commitments. Speculative units can pay interest due. Ponzi units can do neither. When a large number of units are in Ponzi mode, the system breaks down.

When this happens, the authorities usually step in with a list of prescriptions to restore stability, including reducing interest rates, forcing mergers, taking losses onto sovereign balance sheets and writing off debt. However, given developments since 2008, the usual tool box will be severely restricted. The safety net is challenged.

Under a crisis, Central Banks will not be able to slash interest rates by 5% because most rates are already close to 0%. It will not be possible to force mergers as was the case in 2008 given the shortage of quality balance sheets. Opposition to bailouts will be very high given the general level of popular dissatisfaction with the system. This is boosted by current polarization levels. The capacity of sovereign balance sheets to bail out the financial sector will be extremely limited, given the level of debt on sovereign balance sheets following the last round of bailouts. **This is the case for many countries worldwide.**

The net result is most likely to be far more bankruptcies than in 2008.

The time for a system change is overdue.

CONCLUSION

This book has provided you with **high-level insights on how Central Banks decisions and operations affect world markets.**

This book provides **Investors, Chairmen, Chief Executive Officers, Chief Investment Officers, Chief Risk Management Officers, Board Members** with a MUCH clearer understanding of the mistakes that can happen if early signals of financial distress are not detected on time. **Further, this book** provides coherent analysis on how risks evolve to back better hedges and investment decisions!

www.DirectionalAlpha.com

We thank YOU all for claiming the copy of this book about **Central Banks and World Markets** and the REAL truth about how to refine the reading of world markets to avoid mistakes and to improve investment decisions **in order to fulfill the fiduciary duty.**

Have a great day!

www.DirectionalAlpha.com

DISCLAIMER

This material or content is intended to provide general information on the subject, especially on systemic risk, tail risk, volatility, investment, finance, financial modeling only. Neither the author nor publisher provides any legal or other professional advice. If you need professional advice, you should seek advice from the appropriate licensed professional. This report or content does not provide complete information on the subject matter covered. This report is not intended to address specific requirements, either for an individual or an organization. This report or content is intended to be used only as a general guide, and not as a sole source of information on the subject matter. While the author has undertaken diligent efforts to ensure accuracy, there is no guarantee of accuracy or no errors, omissions or typographical errors. Any slights of people or organizations are unintentional. Any reference to any person or organization whether living or dead is purely coincidental. The author *and publisher shall have no liability or responsibility to any person or entity and hereby disclaim all liability, including without limitation, liability for consequential damages regarding any claim, loss or damage that may be incurred, or alleged to have been incurred, directly or indirectly, arising out of the information provided in this report. No part of this material or content may be used, reproduced, distributed or transmitted in any form and by any means whatsoever, including without limitation photocopying, recording or other electronic or mechanical methods or by any information storage and retrieval system, without the prior written permission of the author, except for brief excerpts in a review.*

Use of this content, Directional Alpha, LLC or the www.DirectionalAlpha.com website, and related sites and applications is provided under the www.DirectionalAlpha.com Terms of Use and other Disclaimers posted at www.DirectionalAlpha.com. The information provided in this publication is private, privileged, and confidential information, licensed for your sole individual use as a subscriber and/or purchaser. Directional Alpha, LLC reserves all rights to the content of this publication and related materials. Forwarding, copying, disseminating, or distributing this report in whole or in part, including substantial quotation of any portion the publication or any release of specific investment recommendations, is strictly prohibited. Participation in such activity is grounds for immediate termination of all subscriptions of registered subscribers deemed to be involved at Directional Alpha, LLC's sole discretion, may violate the copyright laws of the United

States of America, and may subject the violator to legal prosecution. Directional Alpha, LLC reserves the right to monitor the use of this publication without disclosure by any electronic means it deems necessary and may change those means without notice at any time. If you have received this publication and are not the intended subscriber or purchaser, please contact us by filling out the contact form located in the contact sections of Directional Alpha, LLC's website: www.DirectionalAlpha.com. Directional Alpha, LLC reserves the right to cancel any subscription at any time, and if it does so, it will promptly refund to the subscriber the amount of the subscription payment previously received relating to the remaining subscription period. Cancellation of a subscription may result from any unauthorized use or reproduction or rebroadcast of any Directional Alpha, LLC publication or website, any infringement or misappropriation of Directional Alpha, LLC's proprietary rights, or any other reason determined in the sole discretion of Directional Alpha, LLC.

This book/report represents an opinion of the authors based on their analysis on the subject. This should be taken and considered for illustrative or educational purpose, which is subject to changes. As such, the reader should consider that it is subject to changes both at present and in the future. The Directional Alpha, LLC website (www.DirectionalAlpha.com), the 360 Pagers or 360 Series, Article Postings, and Blog Postings are published by Directional Alpha, LLC. The information contained in such publications is obtained from sources believed to be reliable, but its accuracy cannot be guaranteed. The *information contained in such publications is not intended to constitute individual investment advice and is not designed to meet your personal financial situation. The opinions expressed in such publications are those of the publisher and are subject to change without notice. The information in such publications may become outdated, and there is no obligation to update any such information. You are advised to discuss with your financial advisers your investment options and whether any investment is suitable for your specific needs prior to making any investments. Further, the analysis and materials contained herein are for informational purposes only and do not constitute legal, financial, tax, accounting or investment advice. The studies and analysis conducted in this document were constructed for illustrative purposes on the basis of knowledge, models, and sources generally accepted by the market practitioners. Its results may differ from the developments of markets, corporate, economic and/or political events at present and/or in the future. Any action and/or decision of any kind based on the use of the information contained in this document are under the sole and only responsibility of the reader/user of this document. The information contained herein is provided "as is" without any express or implied guarantee. The authors of this report or content neither are nor will be liable for damages and/or financial and/or economic direct, indirect, special, consequential, punitive or incidental damages, monetary losses and/or arising and/or related to the use or unauthorized use of the findings, conclusions, and material contained in this report.*

Investing is Inherently Risky: there are risks inherent in all investments, which may make such investments unsuitable for certain persons. These include, for example, economic, political, currency exchange, rate fluctuations, and limited availability of information on international securities. You may lose all of your money on trading and investing. Past performance of an investment is not necessarily indicative of its future results. No assurance can be given that any investment will be profitable or will not be subject to losses. Hypothetical results are reported: results and examples used in the Directional Alpha, LLC's advertisements, books, videos, websites, and other media are, in some cases, based on hypothetical (simulated) financial models and trading models. Hypothetical performance results have certain limitations. Unlike an actual performance record, hypothetical results do not represent actual trading. Hypothetical financial models generally are also subject to the fact that they are designed with the benefit of hindsight. Hypothetical results also do not account for commissions or slippage or different pricing and outcomes.

Information provided by Directional Alpha, LLC is not investment advice. Directional Alpha, LLC is not a registered investment adviser, stock broker, or brokerage. You agree that the Directional Alpha, LLC does not represent, warrant, or take responsibility that any account will or is likely to achieve profit or losses similar to those shown. Examples published by Directional Alpha, LLC are selected for illustrative purposes only. No independent party has audited any hypothetical performance contained in this report, nor has any independent party undertaken to confirm that they reflect the model under the assumptions or conditions specified. Offers disinterested commentary and analysis: Offers disinterested commentary and analysis: Directional Alpha, LLC does not receive any form of payment or other compensation for publishing information, news, research, or any other material concerning specific securities on the network that is intended to affect or influence the value of securities.

Directional Alpha, LLC and other entities in which he has an interest, employees, officers, family, and associates may from time to time have positions in the securities or commodities covered in this report or its website. Directional Alpha, LLC and its management may benefit from an increase or decrease in the share prices of the profiled companies or economic scenarios in any markets. If a particular security featured in a newsletter, report, or publication is concurrently owned by Directional Alpha, LLC in its corporate brokerage account, or in any of the individual accounts of the Directional Alpha, LLC's staff, that fact will be disclosed. Directional Alpha, LLC and its Staff may choose to purchase a security or derivative featured in one of its newsletter publications but typically will wait 3 (three) trading days from the date of publication before initiating said purchase. Company policies are in effect that attempts to avoid potential conflicts of interest and resolve conflicts of interest that do arise in a timely fashion. By using Directional Alpha, LLC's reports and its website and other services provided, you agree not to hold Directional Alpha, LLC, or any of its affiliates, liable for decisions that are based on information contained in blog posts, reader *responses to blog posts, or information anywhere else on their website or in promotional material.*

By using Directional Alpha, LLC's report, and/or content, and/or analyses, and/or website you agree to the Terms of Use, the Privacy Policy, and other Disclaimers posted at Directional Alpha, LLC's website (www.DirectionalAlpha.com). You also agree and accept that these Terms of Use and other Disclaimers will be updated regularly and it is your responsibility to review all updates frequently and on a regular basis by visiting Directional Alpha, LLC website at www.DirectionalAlpha.com.

Copyright © 2017 Directional Alpha, LLC. All rights reserved worldwide.

www.ingramcontent.com/pod-product-compliance
Lightning Source LLC
Chambersburg PA
CBHW050236230526
45470CB00005B/1980